Old ARMAGH

by
Alex F. Young, with photographs from the Des Quail collection

This view of Scotch Street, looking to the Anglican cathedral, gives a clue to its early name, Ferta Street, derived from *Tempall na Ferta*, St Patrick's first church in Armagh. For a time it was Newry Street, and then from around 1661 it was known as Scotland Street due to the number of Scottish settlers living there. This photograph dates from 1909, by which time 'Scotland' had degenerated to 'Scotch'.

Text © Alex F. Young, 2003.
First published in the United Kingdom, 2003,
by Stenlake Publishing,
Telephone / Fax: 01290 551122

ISBN 1 84033 243 3

The publishers regret that they cannot supply
copies of any pictures featured in this book.

ACKNOWLEDGEMENTS
The author wishes to thank Denholm Reid, Des Fitzgerald, Albert Nicholl, John McStravick, W.R. Cardwell of the Royal School, Amanda Moreno of the The Royal Irish Fusiliers Museum, Pat Styles and Pamela Skelly of the National Scout Headquarters Archive, Ella Williamson of The Royal Hibernian Academy, St Patrick's Anglican Cathedral, Armagh, The Irish and Local Studies Library, Armagh, The Sacred Heart Convent, Armagh, Cronan O'Doibhlin and Joe Canning of The Cardinal Tomas O'Fiaich Memorial Library and Archive, Armagh, and Gretta Forster of the Charlemont Arms Hotel, Armagh.

FURTHER READING
The books listed below were used by the author during his research. None of them are available from Stenlake Publishing. Those interested in finding out more are advised to contact their local bookshop or reference library.

Faugh-a-Ballagh, The Regimental Gazette of the 87th Royal Irish Fusiliers, Vol. V No. 48, October 1906.

Guide to St Patrick's Cathedral, Armagh: Historical and Descriptive, Armagh, 1905.

George Bassett, *The Book of County Armagh*, 1888.

Angelique Day and Patrick McWilliams, *Ordnance Survey Memoirs of Ireland, Parishes of County Armagh* (1835–8 ed.), The Institute of Irish Studies, 1990.

Rev W.E.C. Fleming, *Armagh Clergy 1800–2000*, 2001.

Grenfell Morton, *Railways in Ulster*, Friar's Bush Press, 1989.

Theo Snoddy, *Dictionary of Irish Artists (20th Century)*, Wolfhound Press.

Ulster Architectural Heritage Society, *The Buildings of Armagh*, 1992.

The building committee of the Armagh and District Co-operative Society of 1915 consisted of (from left to right): H. Magee, Vice-President; H. Cunningham; J. McCarragher, President; T. Hutchinson; W. Gray, Secretary; and W.W. Moffatt. Trading under the slogan 'All Profits divided', the society traded from premises in Scotch Street until 1960 when it was taken over by the Fane Valley Co-operative Agricultural and Dairying Society. This photograph comes from a correspondence card sent in response to a query – 'Dear Madam, Re: Knitting Machines – Mr Mitchell, Scotch Street, is the only one who keeps them and we would advise you to write him for particulars re same.'

INTRODUCTION

When St Patrick came to *Ard Macha* ('Macha's Height') in AD 444, it had already attained a thousand years of history. But with his decision to establish his church here, it became Ireland's ecclesiastical centre. Fifth century prosperity did not come to Armagh through industry and commerce, but through the growth of the church and its concomitant schools and colleges. Unfortunately, knowledge of its wealth was spread as surely as 'the Word', and between 831 and 1013 'The Isle of Saints and Scholars', and Armagh in particular, was subjected to periodic Viking raids. The twelfth century brought more pillage with the arrival of the Anglo–Normans, and the town found itself in the middle ground between the Norman forces and those of the O'Neills. However, by 1300, Ireland, with the exception of the western fringes, was in Norman hands and, in time, these invaders were assimilated into Irish society.

The Reformation ended two centuries of relative peace in Ireland and marked the passing of the monasteries. For Armagh, built around the Church and monastic life, it had a huge impact which has reverberated down through the centuries. Once again the city was in the front line, as opposing forces see-sawed back and forth.

What the Anglo–Normans had done in the fourteenth century, King James I resorted to in 1608 when he introduced the Plantation scheme, which granted forfeited land to Scottish and English settlers across Ulster. This fomented the 1641 Rebellion in which the Irish, under Sir Phelim O'Neill, fought a losing battle to win back their land. Oliver Cromwell came and went, and the Williamite wars of 1689–90 raged, before peace returned once more.

With peace came Archbishop Robinson, who was appointed Primate in 1765. The sixth son of William Robinson of Rokeby, Yorkshire, he was educated at Westminster School and Christ College, Oxford, graduating in 1733. With his vision of a new Armagh came the Public Library (1771), a new building for the Royal School (1772) and the Observatory (1793).

Armagh missed the worst of the Great Hunger (*An Gorta Mor*) of 1845–52, as potato blight (caused by the fungus *Phytophthora infestans*) swept across Ireland. As the traditional rural staple diet was based on the potato, a million people died and at least a million and a half emigrated.

Although there were a number of weaving mills in and around the town, Armagh was never a true industrial or commercial centre – Portadown carried that mantle. And as isolation diminished with the coming of the railways, what little industry there was soon moved to Belfast.

Over recent decades, the growth of tourism has contributed greatly to local prosperity, although in the late 1920s, while the Rural District Council was debating the question of building Turkish baths as a tourist attraction, one council member declared that he could not think what there was in Armagh for tourists to see!

By virtue of its cathedrals, Armagh was always a city, but only in 1995 was the status officially conferred by the Queen.

St Patrick built a church in Armagh in AD 445, but the layout of the present St Patrick's Anglican Cathedral came with Archbishop O'Scanlain in 1268. It became an Anglican church during the Reformation and a major reconstruction was started by Archbishop Robinson in the eighteenth century. This was completed by Archbishop Beresford in 1834.

Leading from the doorway of St Patrick's Roman Catholic Cathedral, the steps in the foreground run down to Cathedral Road, previously named Mill Street, where it joins Edward Street. The terrace of twenty houses along Edward Street's right side, facing the open area of the Shambles (the common term for a slaughterhouse, which would have been this area's previous use), was built in 1887–88 by George A. Edwards JP for renting to local workers.

Among the changes brought by the Catholic Emancipation Act of 1829 was the return of Roman Catholic archbishops to Armagh. The first appointee was Dr William Crolly. Determined to build a new cathedral, he chose Sallow or Sally Hill as the site and Thomas J. Duff of Newry as the architect. On St Patrick's Day 1840 the foundation stone of the new St Patrick's Roman Catholic Cathedral was laid. Duff planned a south facing, cruciform perpendicular Gothic-style design in Armagh limestone, with a square central tower and two smaller flanking towers. The work halted in 1847 when funds went to famine relief and when the work resumed in 1854 both Crolly and Duff had passed on – the archbishop dying of cholera in 1849. His successor, Dr Joseph Dixon, and the architect J.J. McCarthy, in part abandoned Duff's design and gave the building its distinctive twin spires (each of 210 feet). The building was finally dedicated on 24 August 1873.

Photographed in 1898, four years after it was erected, this memorial to Archbishop Dr Daniel McGettigan (1815–1887) stands in the New Cemetery, with the playing fields of the Diocesan Seminary of St Patrick's College running up to the cathedral. By the late 1880s the old Sandy Hill Cemetery had reached its limits, and in 1889 this eight acre site was secured from St Patrick's and consecrated by Archbishop Logue on Candlemas Day 1890. Dying on 3 December 1887, Archbishop McGettigan was buried at Sandy Hill, but in 1894 his body was transferred to the New Cemetery and placed under this Celtic cross. Standing 24 feet high, it was sculpted by George H. Barnes of Dublin, following designs by William Hague (1836–99), an architect also of Dublin.

Enthroned as Anglican Archbishop of Armagh and Primate of All Ireland on 17 March, 1911, John Baptist Crozier used this photograph on his New Year's greeting card of 1912, 'To wish you every blessing and happiness all through the New Year' .The eldest son of the Rev. Baptist Barton Crozier of Rockview, Ballyhaise, Co. Cavan, he was born in Dublin in 1853 and educated at that city's Trinity College. He died at Armagh on 11 April 1920, and was buried at the cathedral, where a stained-glass window was erected to his memory. Also erected to his memory was the Crozier Hall, attached to St Mark's Church, which was opened in October 1932 by his son Brigadier General B.B. Crozier.

The Courthouse, photographed from the Mall in the summer of 1929, with the war memorial, dedicated the previous December, and the German field guns (removed for recycling in 1940) in position. Built at a cost of £6,000 between 1806 and 1809, and to a design by the Board of Works architect Francis Johnston (1760–1829), this building replaced the County Court House in Market Street. An Armachian, Johnston is remembered for his buildings in Dublin, which include the General Post Office and the Chapel Royal at Dublin Castle.

Lieutenant Colonel Fitzgerald, High Sheriff of the County of Armagh, proclaims the accession of King George V from the steps of the Courthouse on Monday, 16 May 1910. A detachment of the 3rd Battalion Royal Irish Fusiliers, under the command of Captain M.C. Carbery, formed the guard of honour for the event in Armagh. Reporting the event, the *Armagh Guardian* blamed the choice of day for the relatively small crowd – 'Had the day been Saturday or Tuesday [market day] the attendance would have been ten times larger.' What a fine view the spectator on the top corner of the courthouse building had.

The head of the Mall, photographed in 1931, with College Hill coming down from the left and passing the Courthouse, on the right, before rising up College Street to join English Street. Facing the Courthouse is the war memorial, a bronze figure of 'Mourning Victory' by the sculptor C.L. Hartwell, which was dedicated on 3 December 1926.

On the East Mall, the 'superbly regal' late Georgian terrace of Charlemont Place was built between 1827 and 1830 as a speculative venture by Francis William, second Earl of Charlemont, to a design by the architect William Murray. Nos. 1–4 were originally valued at £60 and No. 5 (extreme right) at £65. Although extensively damaged by a 500 lb bomb in April 1989, restoration work has returned it to the condition it was in when this photograph was taken in 1903. Beyond, the eleven houses of Beresford Row, built between 1819 and 1840, commemorate Lord John George Beresford, Archbishop of Armagh (1822–62), and take East Mall to its junction with College Hill.

The Mall West, with the Anglican cathedral on the hill and the Masonic Hall and the First Armagh Presbyterian Church behind the trees. Built in 1884, at a cost of £1,400, the early-Gothic style Masonic Hall was designed by James H. Fullerton. At one time it was home to Lodges Nos.39, 299, 400 and 623, but it is no longer used for this purpose. On the corner of Russell Street, the First Presbyterian Church was built in 1878 to a design by the architects Young & McKenzie.

The Mall Walk (West), photographed on a summer's afternoon in 1909. The Mall was granted to the people of Armagh in 1797 by Primate Newcombe, when its perimeter was a racecourse and its centre a swamp. However, drainage and improvements transformed it into 'a public walk for the people'. It has also served as a cricket pitch, a rugby pitch, a site for a bandstand and home to the memorials and trophies of war.

The south side of College Street as it runs from the Mall to Upper English Street. Rocque's 1760 map shows it as 'the road to Castle Dillon', home of the Molyneaux family, out on the Portadown road. Built in the 1820s, this terrace is likened to Beresford Row on the opposite side of the Mall.

In 1587 Queen Elizabeth I granted a patent to Hugh Roe O'Neill, Earl of Tyrone, to hold a market in Armagh. The Market House, to the right of this 1905 photograph, was built much later. As can be seen by the potato and turnip filled carts, this Tuesday market was for produce. Other markets were held in Irish Street (for flax), Dobbin Street (poultry, eggs and butter), the Shambles in Mill Street (grain, grass seed and pork) and in Gaol Square (live pigs).

Market Street, opposite the Market House, photographed in the 1930s. Of the shop premises, Whitsitt Bros. was a wholesale and retail ironmonger and hardware merchant, while T.J. Walker was a draper. The lorry belonged to Thomas Moore the wholesale wine and spirit merchant, whose bonded warehouse was in Dobbin Street.

Market Square in 1936. The Market House, on the left, was built in 1815 on the site occupied by the Session House and the first Gaol (which was replaced by the one in the Mall). In 1912, when it became Armagh Municipal Technical School, a third storey was added. Zwecker's barber's shop on the far corner was opened by Theodore Zwecker in 1902 and closed in 1972.

This and the following photograph show the annual Armagh Trade Exhibition of 1913, which was held in the Market House. Among the local exhibitors can be seen the draper, W.J. Lennox (est. 1867) of Market Square, and James Irwin's City Bakery of Scotch Street.

The exhibition drew both local and national companies, including White, Tomkins & Courage, the oatmeal manufacturer from Belfast. Luckily the photographer was early enough to beat the crowds. The event did not resume after the First World War.

Upper English Street, photographed in 1936 when F.W. Woolworth was in its first year after taking over the shop of Couser, the grocer and provision merchant. Next on the right is the Ulster Bank, which was once Adams's Wool Shop, followed by the Beresford Arms Hotel. Built for the Reverend Nathaniel Whalley in 1717, this property began its career as a hotel around 1769 when it was known as The King's Head. In 1792 it was The Molyneux Arms, in 1808 The King's Arms, in 1824 The Royal Hibernian, and by 1844 it had become the Beresford. It suffered bomb damage in 1972.

As businesses have come and gone in English Street, the Charlemont Arms Hotel has thrived through the centuries. It was originally home to a Dr Atkinson, but had become a hostelry – The Caulfield Arms – by the 1760s. In 1763 it was renamed when the fourth Viscount Caulfield was created Earl of Charlemont. For many years John Hughes was the host, but an advertisement in Bassett's *The Book of County Armagh* (1888) gives the proprietor as J.H. Mann, 'late of London and Glasgow', who offered accommodation 'in the best business centre . . . remodelled and refurnished throughout'. Following Mann's departure in 1906, there were a number of owners, before the Forster family took over in 1934. They have worked through an ongoing programme of improvements ever since. Collins's survives as a newsagent and confectioner, and a descendant of McStravick the saddler is now a solicitor in the premises.

Post Office 'Square' in 1909, with, running to the left, Mitchell the draper, the City Medical Hall and, at an angle, the Belfast Bank (later the Northern Bank), which was built in 1851 to a design by Charles Lanyon. Angled on the corner is the Armagh Guardian office and printworks. Built around 1905, this post office replaced a predecessor in Russell Street, but was itself demolished in the 1960s.

By 1931 the greatest change on the street is the dominance of the motor car and the arrival of motor dealers, in this case Gilbert Sleator, who was the Armagh agent for Rover Cars.

By the time of this 1938 photograph the centrally situated gas lamp (shown on the front cover photograph), a popular meeting place and cab stance, had gone, as well as most of the horse-drawn vehicles. The overhead telephone lines had also increased in quantity. Could the crowd gathered at College Street corner really have just been watching the painter?

The Tontine Assembly Rooms in English Street were built in the 1790s and contained a hall with seating for up to 500 people and other rooms and offices, some of which were let to the Town Commissioners. In 1908 Armagh Urban District Council took over and refurbished the building for their offices. It was demolished in 1972, following an explosion.

Later captured in John Luke's 1945 painting 'The Old Callan Bridge', this photograph of the four span hump-backed Callan Bridge was taken in 1898. Dating from the fourteenth century, the bridge carried the main road to the west. On the hill to the right is the Windmill, built around 1810 as a flour grinding mill to replace an earlier windmill which had been erected in the seventeenth century. It was defunct by the 1850s but still stands, minus its sails.

Armagh Railway Station, photographed in the 1920s. The first passenger train to Armagh arrived from Portadown on the Ulster Railway's line on 1 March 1848, but it was another ten years before the service could continue to Monaghan. The next line to open was the Newry and Armagh Railway to Goraghwood in 1864 and this was followed in 1910 by the Castleblaney, Keady and Armagh Railway. Lecturing on 'Armagh since 1757' to Armagh Parliamentary and Debating Society in January 1914, Mr J.C. McBride (presumably a local historian) meandered through old streets, old families and the first railways, of which he said, 'The railway station used to be . . .[run by] the Ulster Railway and if the present generation could have seen it they would think it a miserable place.' Obviously, things had improved by the time this photograph was taken.

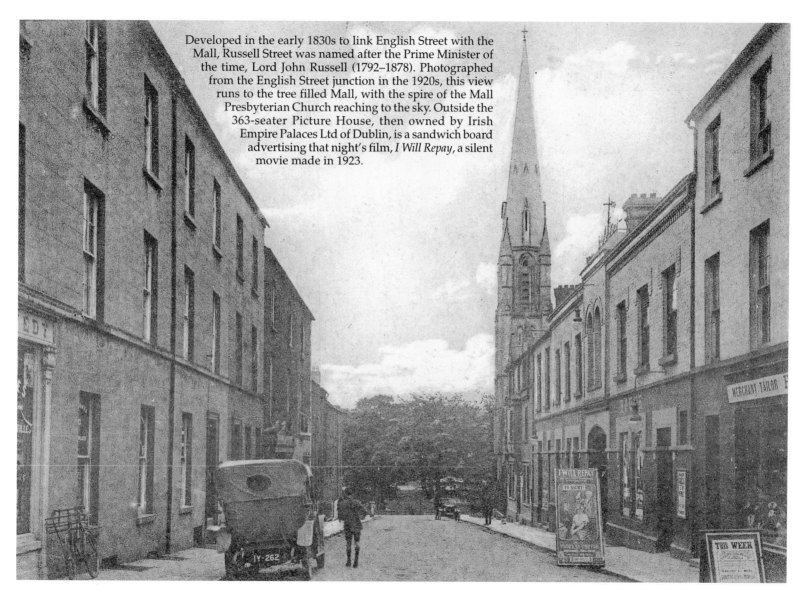

Developed in the early 1830s to link English Street with the Mall, Russell Street was named after the Prime Minister of the time, Lord John Russell (1792–1878). Photographed from the English Street junction in the 1920s, this view runs to the tree filled Mall, with the spire of the Mall Presbyterian Church reaching to the sky. Outside the 363-seater Picture House, then owned by Irish Empire Palaces Ltd of Dublin, is a sandwich board advertising that night's film, *I Will Repay*, a silent movie made in 1923.

With Ogle Street, Thomas Street was opened in 1759 as a 'ring road' to bypass the incline of Cathedral Hill. Their names derive from Thomas Ogle who had a marble polishing mill in the vicinity.

In the quarter century since the photograph on page 1 was taken, the most striking change to Scotch Street is the horizontal stripe pattern given to the print works of the *Ulster Gazette* (established in 1844) and *Armagh Standard*.

Scotch Street, looking towards Barrack Street in the summer of 1952. Shops and businesses stand shoulder to shoulder, with the *Ulster Gazette* office, on the right, standing out. Equally eye-catching was the golden teapot of the City Bakery Café above Irwin's. In its early days steam curled out from teapot's spout. James Irwin's business as a baker, provision merchant and grocer started in 1874 and was bought by J.P. McVitty in 1921. The premises closed in the late 1940s and the site was redeveloped in the early 1980s.

A farm lad, thought to be Frank Mallon, leads his donkey and cart along St Catherine's Alley, towards the farm attached to the Convent of the Sacred Heart. Founded in France in 1800 to educate children of the aristocracy following the Revolution and the 'Reign of Terror', the nuns came to Armagh in 1851 and opened a school in Abbey Street, before moving to Charlemont Place. The foundation stone of this convent was laid on 30 April 1857.

Named after Armagh's original barracks – built in 1736 and demolished in 1780 to make way for the Gaol – Barrack Street runs from Scotch Street to the end of the Mall.

Built in 1773, Gough Barracks were named in honour of Field Marshall Hugh Gough, first Viscount Gough. During the Peninsular War of the early nineteenth century he commanded the 2nd battalion of the 87th Regiment of Foot against the French Army at the Battle of Barossa. These were the earliest purpose-built barracks in Ulster (the earlier barracks had probably been adapted from buildings erected for other purposes).

In the shadow of the Anglican cathedral, the public library in Abbey Street was opened in 1771. Originally this face on Abbey Street was three bay, but was extended to five in 1845. Described as 'one of the most perfect architectural set pieces in the city', the library was established by a parliamentary Act instigated by Archbishop Robinson, and was built to a plan by the architect Thomas Cooley (1740–1784).

Mr Henry Hirsch (centre) with the staff and pupils of the Royal School in 1910. After eight years at Campbell College, Belfast, the Cambridge-educated Glaswegian was appointed Headmaster of the Royal School in 1904. Having played rugby, soccer and cricket as a student for Christ College, it is not surprising to find him with Royal School teams in the following photographs. Retiring in 1929, he died at Armagh in January 1949. No others in the photograph can be named, but his son, C.E.R. Hirsch (a future brigadier and British liaison officer in South Africa in 1949), and his three daughters may be in the group. Originally opened in 1772, to the fee-paying parents of these boys the Royal School would have been the epitome of the English public school. Today, with the status of a voluntary grammar school, this elitism has gone, and although still founded in the Church of Ireland, it is a non-denominational school with a Christian ethos.

The Boy Scout movement came to Northern Ireland in 1907, starting in Belfast within the Boys' Brigade and the Young Men's Christian Association. The 1st Armagh Group was the thirty-sixth founded within Ireland, but as records are scant, it is unknown when this 'sponsored group' within the Royal School was formed. Surviving with this photograph, are the boys surnames. Standing left to right are Enshaw, Leeman, Waddell II, Cartmill, Moeran I, Morrison, Wallace III, Martin, and Moeran II; while sitting are Stewart II, Little IV, Turner I, Strong I, Mr Boddington (Scout Master), Strong II, Oram, Turner II, and Towe. On the ground are Kelly III, Mouritz, Brooks, Hirsch, Olton I and II, and Murphy (in those days boys were not referred to by their first names; instead Roman numerals were attached to their surnames to identify individual boys with a common surname).

Cricket started at the Royal School in 1905, with G.A. Edwards as captain. No names survive for the members of this team, photographed in 1910, but C.S. Marriott, who was at that time a pupil and who went on to play for Kent County Cricket Club and England, may be one of them.

The cricket team going through their programme of 'Swedish Drill' in the early 1900s. Devised by the Swede, Per Henrik Ling (1776–1839), the drill sought to attain all-round physical development through harmonious exercises.

The 1915 Royal School rugby team, or 'Footer team' as it is inscribed in the album from which these photographs come. Standing left to right, are Bryson I, Fellows II, Christie, Mr Hirsch, Bebe, McClenaghan II, and Lindsay; while sitting are McMahon, Fellows I, Bates, Kelly I, Irwin, Strong II, and McClenaghan I. On the ground are Best I and Holland I. Those in white were also Ulster team members.

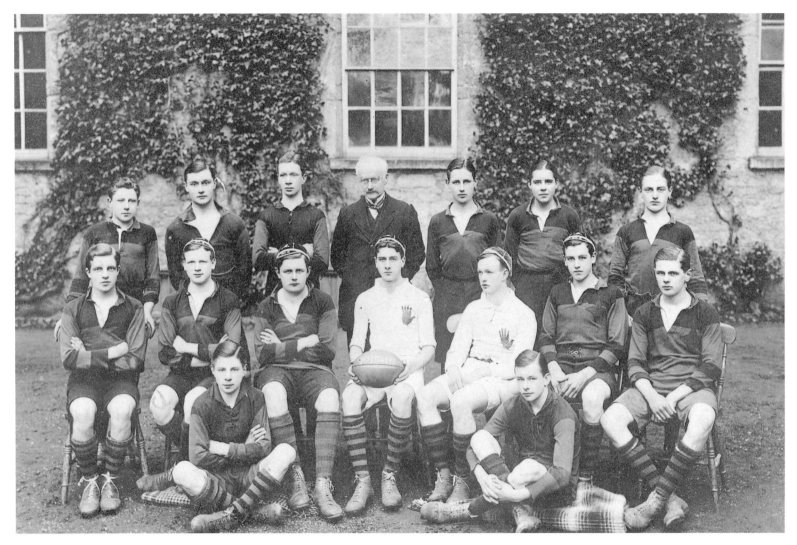

The 'Footer team' of the following year, 1916. Standing, left to right, are Dobbin, McConnell I, Bowen, Mr Hirsch, Shackleton, Moeran I, and Little IV; while sitting are Bryson I, Lindsay, Fellows I, Strong II, Bebe, Christie, and Fellows II. On the ground are Enshaw and Simpson.

The Second Team for the season of 1916. Standing, left to right, are Shackleton, Rynd, Dobbin, Morrison, Howe, Patterson, and McCrindle I; while sitting are Turner II, Moeran I, Little IV, Strong I, Enshaw, Simpson, and Deans. On the ground are Martin II and Stewert II.

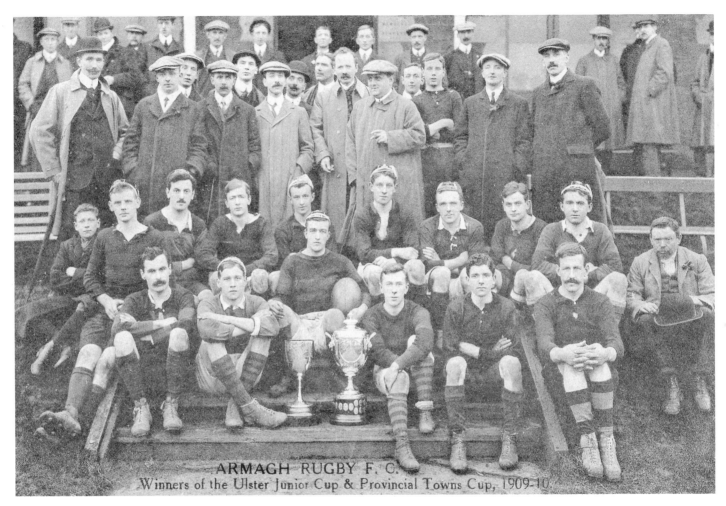

ARMAGH RUGBY F. C.
Winners of the Ulster Junior Cup & Provincial Towns Cup, 1909-10.

Armagh Rugby Football Club, photographed at the Ormeau Ground, Belfast, on 2 April 1910, after beating Carrick to win the Provincial Towns' Cup. Founded in 1875, ten years before the establishment of the northern branch of the Irish Rugby Football Union, they played on the Mall before moving to the Palace Demesne. This team consisted of, back row (left to right) – W.A. Burgess, P.A. Watson, J.B. Whitsitt, J.I. Lea, R.V.E. Walsh, G. Deacon, W.E. Andrews, and C.E. Watson; front row – J. Wilton, W.B. Sproule, R. Whitsitt (Captain), P. Huston, S.C.L. Walsh, G. Binns (Secretary), with A.R. Nunns standing in the group behind. Sitting to the extreme right (with the hat on his knee) is H. Thomas, a retired player.

Sir Edward Carson and his entourage, photographed outside the Royal School, College Hill, on Saturday, 4 October 1913, having stopped to review a march past before going to the Deanery. They had come from Portadown the previous evening and spent the morning touring Armagh by carriage. A lawyer and MP for Dublin, Sir Edward (1854–1935) was leader of the Irish Unionist Party from 1910 and organised the Ulster Volunteers in the opposition to Home Rule. In a distinguished legal career he held the posts of Solicitor-General for Ireland (1892) and for England (1900–06), Attorney-General (1915), and was First Lord of the Admiralty in 1917.

With the public library in Abbey Street, the observatory on College Hill was another of Primate Richard Robinson's projects of the late 1700s, designed to give Armagh 'an environment of cultured serenity and good taste' and to help establish it as a university town. While the former was no doubt achieved, the establishment of a university did not come to pass.